So Far...

12 INTROSPECTIVE PIECES
COMPOSED BY PHILLIP KEVEREN

— PIANO LEVEL —
INTERMEDIATE TO EARLY ADVANCED

ISBN 978-1-70513-711-6

HAL•LEONARD®
——— A Muse Group Company ———

Visit Hal Leonard Online at
www.halleonard.com

Visit Phillip at
www.phillipkeveren.com

World headquarters, contact:
Hal Leonard
7777 West Bluemound Road
Milwaukee, WI 53213
Email: info@halleonard.com

In Europe, contact:
Hal Leonard Europe Limited
Dettingen Way
Bury St Edmunds, Suffolk, IP33 3YB
Email: info@halleonardeurope.com

In Australia, contact:
Hal Leonard Australia Pty. Ltd.
4 Lentara Court
Cheltenham, Victoria, 3192 Australia
Email: info@halleonard.com.au

PREFACE

"Decade" birthdays get our attention. I have not been that impressed with any of mine, until this one. Six decades. It seems like a good time to take stock and be grateful. In that spirit, I have written twelve new piano compositions, musical timestamps from my life's journey.

SO FAR...

Memories and milestones
What we've seen
What we've dreamed
So far...

Pacific Moonlight. I married a Southern California girl. The scent of ocean spray, the glory of a radiant sunset, the exhilaration of a "perfect wave" – all these memories are weaved in the tapestry of our courtship.

Fireflies. I did not really understand the magic of fireflies until we moved to Tennessee. Their delicate glistening in the darkness is a nocturnal treat to behold.

Sage. I was born in the high desert of Eastern Oregon. It is vast, spacious, wide-open country. The scent of sagebrush is overwhelming, and it will forever live in my memory. It is particularly pungent after a summer thunderstorm, lingering in the air with such intensity that you can almost taste it.

Nazo (Enigma). I spent a great deal of time in my 20s and 30s working in Japan. I love the people of this beautiful country. I love their food and admire their culture. I came to recognize that I would never completely understand many things about this mysterious place. Hence, the title of the piece translates (as closely as possible) to *enigma*.

Greener Pastures. "Turning the page" on our Southern California chapter was a big decision on so many levels. However, Nashville did not disappoint. The natural beauty of the area, combined with a music community like no other, has made for a sweet life. This is my ode to "Music City."

Isn't It Grand? My first year of college was an immersion in jazz. I fell in love with the harmonic colors of the genre. This composition is written in the "Great American Songbook" style that Irving Berlin, George Gershwin, Jerome Kern, Duke Ellington – and a few other gifted writers – gave to the world. This melody is in search of a lyric. Ira, are you listening?

Regrets. When I hear people say, reflecting on their life: "I have no regrets"—I do not believe them. I think every life has regrets, and I certainly have mine. My desire has been to learn from mistakes, but not to wallow in their memory.

Turning the Page. Knowing when to move on is one of life's most difficult lessons. Have I "stayed too long at the fair," or do I need to buckle in and ford another stream?

Second Chance. Grandparenthood is a unique opportunity to revisit the joys and travails of raising children. The learned lessons of life color the experience in a very special way. This lullaby is dedicated to our cherished grandkids—Charlie John and Ellie Kate—as well as souls we've yet to meet.

Steadfast. My wife, Lisa, has stood with me through good times and bad. She is the most loyal person I have ever known, and a blessing beyond measure.

Infinity. Gazing into the night sky is one of life's most inspiring and humbling experiences. When I see the moon and the stars, I think of all they have seen from their rarified view in the heavens: all that has come before us, and all that will follow our short sojourn on earth.

Simplicity is the final achievement. After one has played a vast quantity of notes and more notes, it is simplicity that emerges as the crowning reward of art.

– Frédéric Chopin

June 2021

Phillip's recording of *So Far...*,
released on the Burton Avenue Music label,
is available on all digital platforms.

...with the London Symphony Orchestra at Abbey Road

...in the studio

CONTENTS

To Dave Grusin

So Far...

By Phillip Keveren

Reflectively, freely

p

With pedal

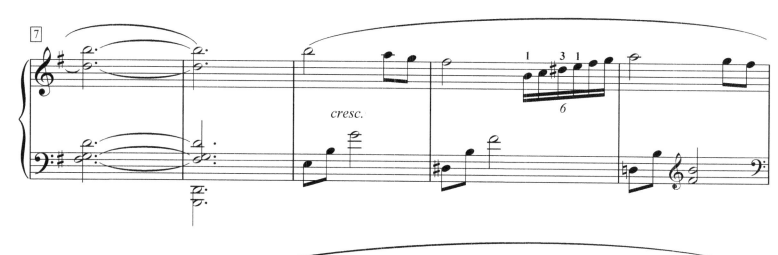

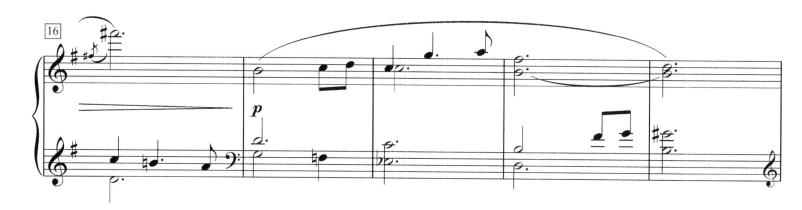

To Robert Linn

Pacific Moonlight

By Phillip Keveren

To Lindsay & Sean

Fireflies

By Phillip Keveren

To Aaron Copland

Sage

By Phillip Keveren

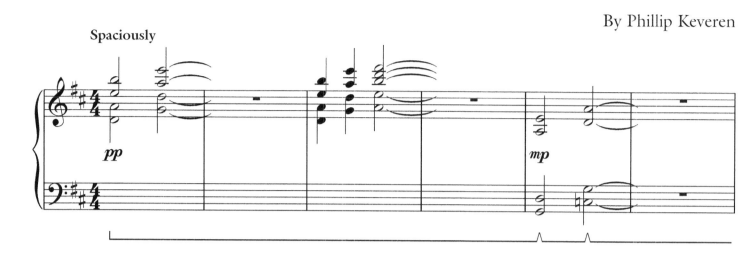

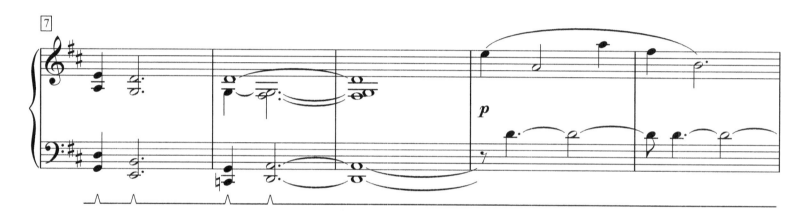

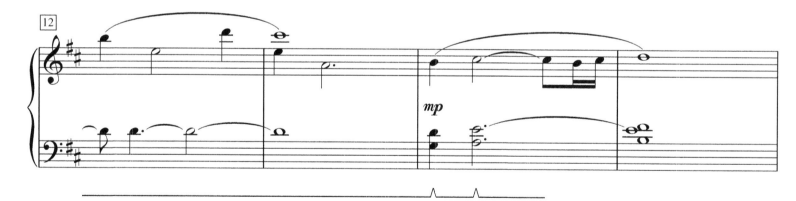

To Akira

Nazo
(Enigma)

By Phillip Keveren

Veiled ♩ = c. 88

With pedal

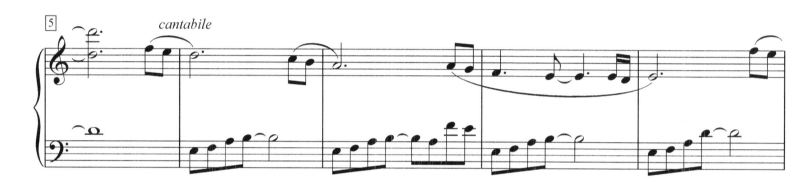

To Hoop

Greener Pastures

By Phillip Keveren

Contented ♩ = c. 63

p

With pedal

mp

To Hal, Larry, and The Players

Isn't It Grand?

By Phillip Keveren

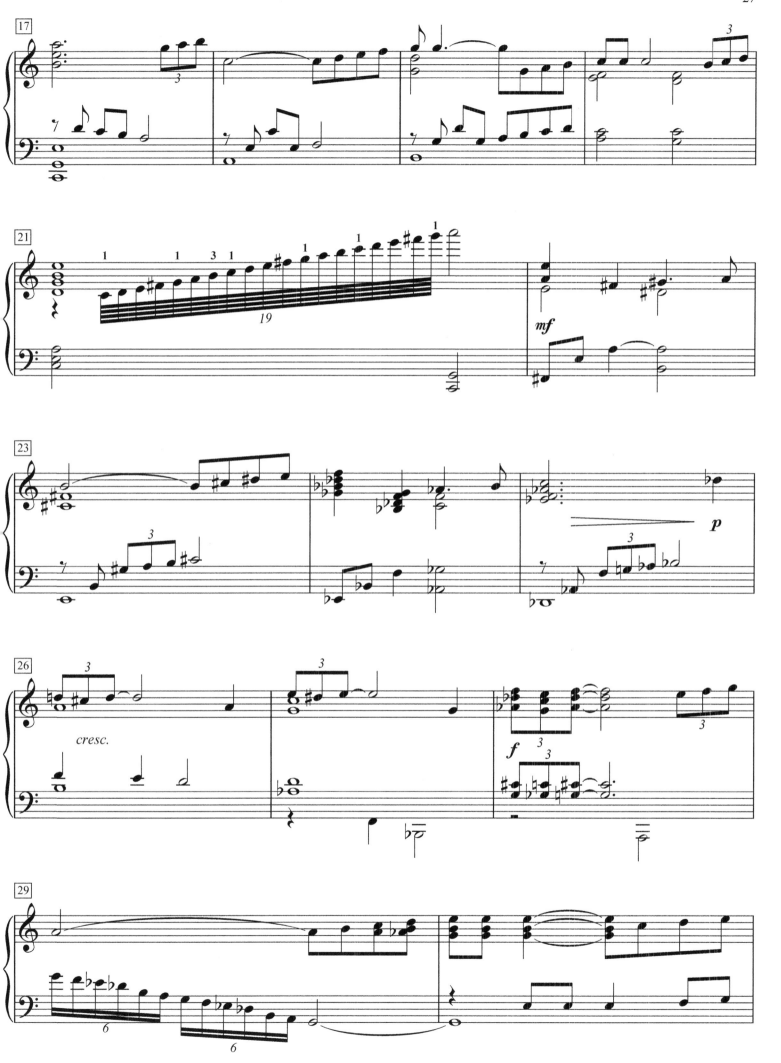

To John Williams

Regrets

By Phillip Keveren

To Karen, Fern & Debbie

Turning the Page

By Phillip Keveren

With motion ♩ = 134

Pedal liberally

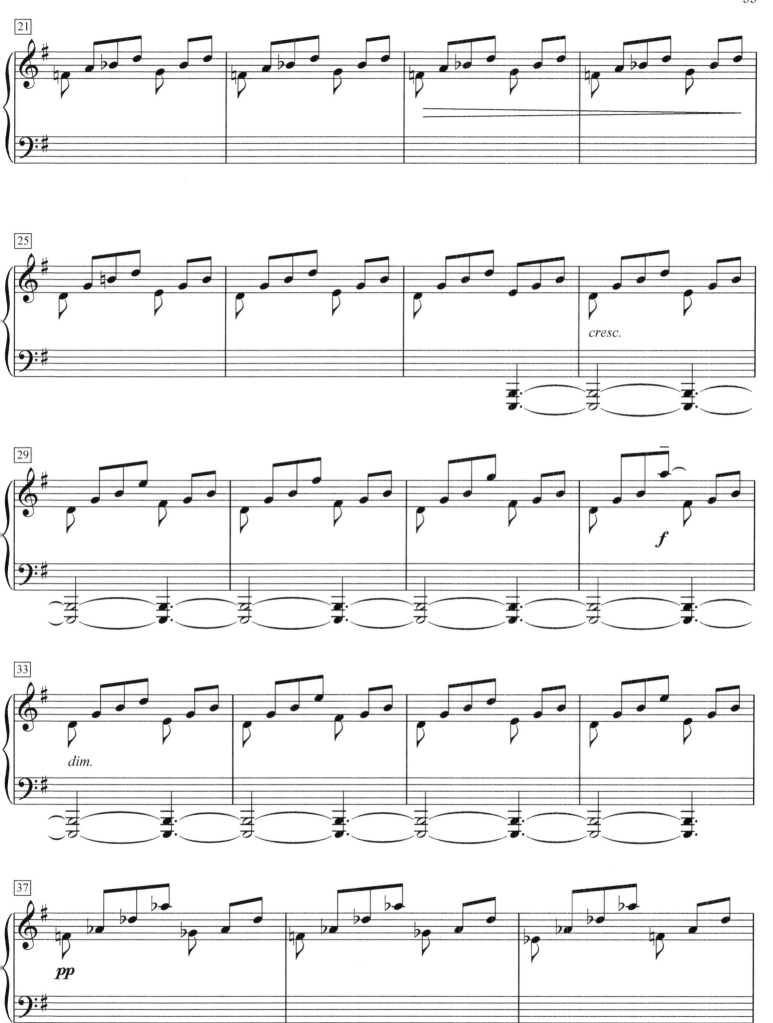

To our Grandchildren

Second Chance
(A Lullaby)

By Phillip Keveren

To Lisa

Steadfast

By Phillip Keveren

Rubato

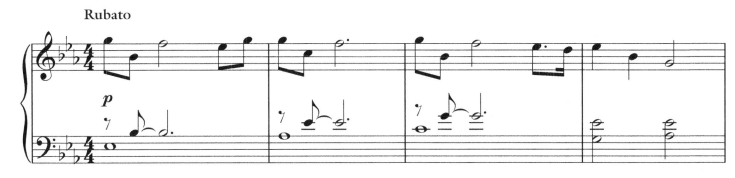

With pedal

To the Great I Am

Infinity

By Phillip Keveren

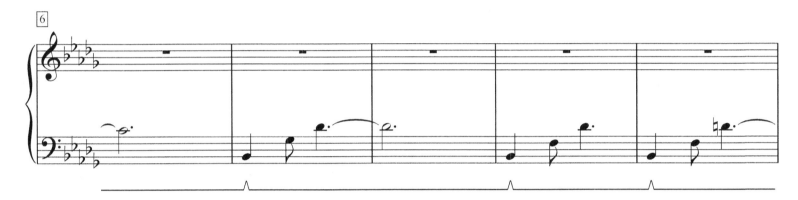

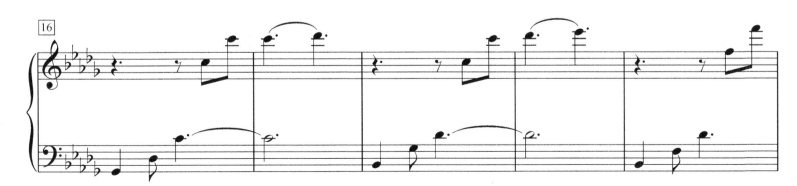

...Family

...Steadfast

...and the beat goes on

ALSO BY PHILLIP KEVEREN

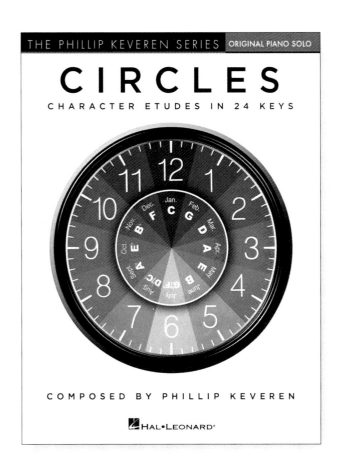

HL 301857 CIRCLES

24 character etudes representing all of the 12 major and minor keys. These original solos range widely in emotion and was inspired by the calendar months from the viewpoint of life in the northern hemisphere (where Keveren grew up). May be performed as a set, in selected keys, or individually.

HL 300640 PIANO CALM

An engaging collection of original piano solos intended to elevate performer and listener into a meditative, peaceful state of mind. Titles: Alpine Meadow • By the Pond • Dawn • Dreaming • Floating • Frosted Windowpane • Gentle Breeze • Hush • Johann's Music Box • Lavender • Nightfall • Peaceful Stream • Pianissimo • Rain • Winter Sky. A recording is available via Burton Avenue Music.